MINING COAL

JOHN DAVEY

A & C Black London

Fossil fern found in coal. You can read more about fossils in *Life before Man* in the same series

Old style pit head in Staffordshire

Published by A & C Black Ltd
35 Bedford Row London WC1R 4JH

ISBN 0 7136 1596 6

© A & C Black Ltd 1976

First published 1976

Filmset and printed in Great Britain by
BAS Printers Limited, Wallop, Hampshire

Contents

Gathering sea coal (see page 45)

Acknowledgements

The author and publishers are grateful to the following for permission to reproduce photographs:

Associated Electrical Industries Ltd 21a; Central Electricity Generating Board 60c; Crown Copyright 31b, 54a; Irish Peat Development Authority 43b; Mary Evans Picture Library 45a, 49a, b, c; The Executors of Sir Harold Wernher 44b; Huwood Ltd 21b; Museum of English Rural Life 43a; National Coal Board 1, 2a, b, 3, 4a, b, 5a, b, 6a, 7a, b, 8a, b, 9, 10a, b, 11a, b, 14a, b, 15a, b, 16a, b, 17a, b, 19a, b, 20, 22, 23b, 24b, 25a, b, c, 26b, c, 27a, b, 28a, b, c, 29a, b, 30, 31a, 32, 33a, b, 34, 35, 36a, 37, 38a, b, 39a, b, c, 41a, b, 42a, 44a, 46a, 47b, 48a, b, 50, 51a, b, c, 52b, 53a, b, 54b, 55, 56a, b, 57b, 58, 59, 60a, b, 61a, b, 62, 63a, b; NCK Rapier Ltd 57a; Northern Echo 45b; North of England Newspapers (Westminster Press Ltd) 40; Derek Peters 50a; Science Museum 46b, 47a; Topical Press Agency Ltd 6b, 21b.
All other line drawings by Technical Art Services Ltd.

The author would like to thank W Tatham, NCB Safety Officer, and H Hughes, MRDE, for their assistance in the preparation of this book.

The main roadway of Daw Mill Colliery, Warwickshire

At the coal face

1 Mining today

Coal is one of the most valuable and important materials in the world. It is far more useful to us than gold, for instance, or than any of the precious stones like diamonds or rubies.

In Britain, everyone relies to a large degree on coal for warmth, light and power. More than half the coal that is mined is used to produce electricity for homes, streets and factories. In addition, hundreds of substances called *by-products* are made from coal. They range from aspirins and soap to road tar, plastics and paint.

How is this most valuable material dug out of the earth? What is it like to work in a coal mine? What are the various jobs that have to be done far below the earth's surface and why is mining looked upon as one of the hardest and most dangerous ways of earning a living?

Newly-made Phurnacite—a popular boiler fuel

Clocking in at the lamp cabin

Filling dudleys before going on shift

The miner goes to work

At a coal mine the *pit head* is the name for the group of buildings clustering round the mouths of the two great shafts. Here on the surface, two tall towers (the winding houses) mark the position of the shafts. There are buildings where the coal is washed and processed, workshops, offices, power houses, locker rooms and baths.

The miner arrives at the pit head in his ordinary street clothes and gets ready to go down the mine. He goes first to the 'clean end' of the pithead baths. Here he leaves his clothes in his clean locker and with only his towel, his *snap* tin (which keeps his food for the day fresh, airtight and vermin-proof) and his *dudley* (drinking bottle) he walks to his dirty clothes locker. He puts on his working clothes, his pit helmet, his steel-capped safety boots, protective gloves (and possibly kneepads) and walks over to the lamp cabin to collect his electric lamp, which has been automatically re-charged on a rack of battery chargers.

Walking to the shaft at Houghton colliery

Inside the cage

He probably meets a number of his workmates and they go to the shaft together. If they are working together as a team they may well look out for their mates of the previous shift who are just coming up the pit. The previous shift will give a quick report on how they left their work down below, whether there were any hold-ups or whether they had run into bad conditions.

The work of the mine is divided into three main shifts, the Morning, Afternoon and Night shifts, though there are overlapping shifts for craftsmen, electricians, fitters and so on.

At the shaft the miners have to take their turn; hundreds of men cannot arrive at the pit bottom together. In groups of fifteen or twenty on both decks of the *cage* (right) they prepare to go down the mine.

The banksman checks each man to make sure he is not carrying matches or a cigarette lighter

A modern pit head. The winding gear is now enclosed in towers

First of all the *banksman*, who is in charge of the cage at the pit top, checks that they are not carrying any matches or cigarette lighters which could cause a fire in the mine.

Each miner leaves his own *tally*, a numbered metal disc, with the banksman. This is sent back to the Surface Control room and is returned to him when he hands in his lamp at the end of the shift. This disc is very important. If a serious disaster took place it could be the only way the rescuers would know whether he was still in the workings. Each miner carries a second disc, usually attached to the battery on his lamp, so that if he leaves the pit by another exit in an emergency there is yet another record of his whereabouts.

When all is ready the banksman signals to the winding engine man. The *onsetter*, who is in charge of the cage at the pit bottom, signals when the pit bottom cage is ready with men waiting to come up. The banksman releases a lever, and the cage drops down into the darkness.

There is very little light (only the light of the men's cap lamps) and just a slight rattling noise as the cage moves between the steel ropes which guide it.

As one cage reaches the bottom the other cage arrives at the pit top and the men stumble out into the sunshine, their day's work done. They head for the lamp cabin (where the lamps are recharged) the pit head baths and then probably the pit canteen for a meal before they make for home.

The pit head baths

Loaded trucks at the pit bottom

Down the mine

The pit bottom is brightly lit and white-washed with a high arched concrete roof, rather like a London Tube station. In the pit bottom area there is an office, with tables, telephones, report forms and writing materials. From here the Undermanager directs operations. He is in touch with all parts of the mine and with the Manager, who is usually on the surface except when he comes down the pit for a daily tour of inspection of any trouble spots.

Engine rooms, diesel *stables*, steel presses for straightening bent girders and maintenance shops are all found in this area. They are built within the region known as the *shaft pillar*. This is an area around the base of the shafts from which no coal has been taken. The ground is stable and unlikely to move. Any movement in the shafts would, of course, be disastrous. The shaft pillar extends from the pit bottom out towards the workings a distance of approximately half the depth of the shaft.

On arriving at the pit bottom the miner probably checks with his 'deputy' (foreman) who is in charge of a *district* of the pit. He finds out what needs to be done and goes off to his appointed place.

Supplies (mainly roof supports) being carried from the pit bottom to the working area

A special train carries the miners towards the coal face

Pipe fitters, electricians, rope men, and diesel maintenance men are not attached to just one district and they report to their own foremen.

For the others, the coal face where the coal is actually being cut may be as much as five kilometres away and so they board a special train and are transported part of the way to the face. Men and materials are not carried together in case of accidents, and the 'paddy trains' are very like open-air carriages that you may have travelled on at the seaside.

Away from the pit bottom the overhead lights are left behind and the only light comes from the men's cap lamps and the headlight of the diesel, stabbing through the darkness. The driver stops the train at stations, where the tunnel is white-washed and sometimes well lit.

The miner usually has to walk the last 1.5 to 2 km to the coal face, because the diesel train rarely goes right up to the face.

A conveyor belt runs along the side of the *gate* (tunnel) leading to the coal face. At the end of the gate the roof suddenly lowers, and here is the *face lip* where the coal is cut from the face.

The conveyor belt from the coal face. The miners have to walk at this point

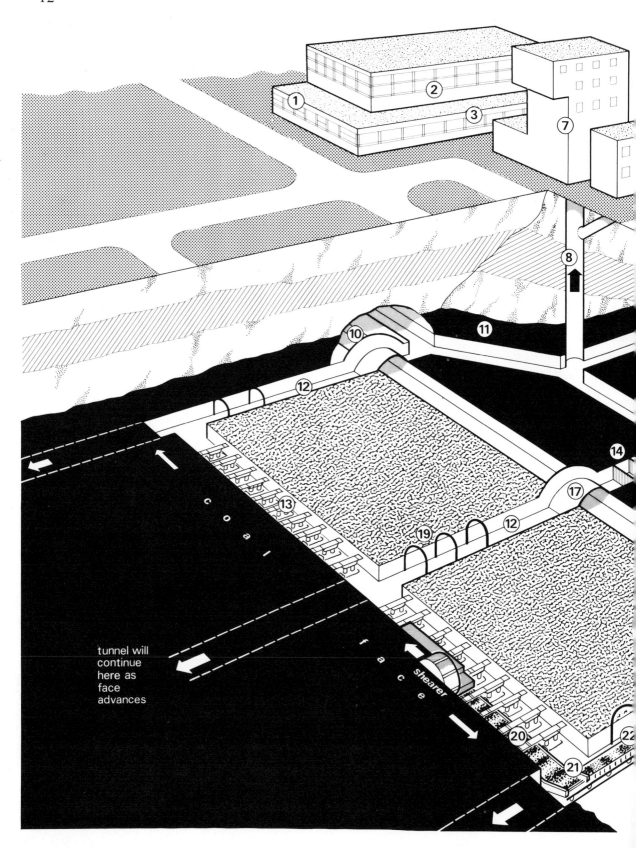

tunnel will
continue
here as
face
advances

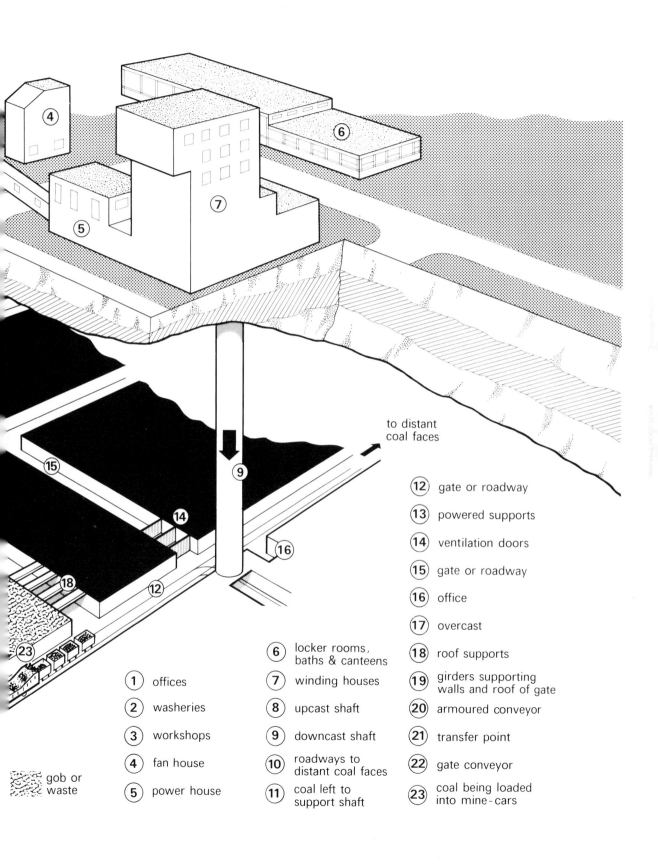

to distant
coal faces

(12) gate or roadway

(13) powered supports

(14) ventilation doors

(15) gate or roadway

(16) office

(17) overcast

(18) roof supports

(19) girders supporting
walls and roof of gate

(20) armoured conveyor

(21) transfer point

(22) gate conveyor

(23) coal being loaded
into mine-cars

(1) offices

(2) washeries

(3) workshops

(4) fan house

(5) power house

(6) locker rooms,
baths & canteens

(7) winding houses

(8) upcast shaft

(9) downcast shaft

(10) roadways to
distant coal faces

(11) coal left to
support shaft

gob or
waste

2 The coal face

It is very hot, dusty and noisy at the coal face. There is not very much light, only the miners' cap lamps shining through the gloom. The miners work here in a confined space, operating the huge machines which are used to cut the coal from the coal *seam*.

A seam is a band of rock, in this case coal, which runs at a similar level through the earth's crust like the layer of jam in a sponge cake. The average worked seam in British mines is 1.5 metres in height.

The coal face is a wall of rock, usually about 160 metres long, with a band of coal running through it. Three roadways (tunnels) are cut into this wall; one at each end and one in the middle. These roadways are at least twice as high as the coal seam itself, to make room for men and machinery to get to the seam.

A slice of coal is extracted along the seam between the tunnels. After each slice has been taken, the tunnels and the coal-cutting machinery advance into the wall of rock to take another cut. This is called *long wall* mining. The roof over the seam is then allowed to collapse. The high roof of the tunnels, however, is supported by girders.

This man is working a modern cutting machine called a trepanner under a hydraulic roof support

The old way—'holing under'. The collier undercut the coal before hacking it down and loading by hand into tubs

Trepanner at Manton colliery, Yorkshire

Extracting the coal

Coal is removed from the seam, slice by slice, by a cutting machine. As it moves along the face, the machine shovels the coal on to an *armoured belt* running alongside. An armoured belt consists of a steel chain with interlinking metal plates. It is very strong and carries a stream of coal along to the end of the face.

There are several types of cutting or shearing machine but they all do a similar job. In a *trepanner*, short picks about eight centimetres long are set in a circular drum which revolves at great speed and cuts a core through the coal. A machine which shears a slice off the wall of coal is called a *shearer loader*.

Mechanical picks have replaced thirty or forty men who in the past attacked the coal face with pick and shovel and explosives, after a cutting machine had undercut the face for them. Each man had his 'stint' or fixed number of yards and each placed props and overhead metal bars to protect himself from falling stone in the new space which he had hollowed out.

A shearer loader at Kellingley colliery, Yorkshire

As the cutting machine travels down the face, coal is deposited onto the conveyor belt

The man in charge of the cutting machine cuts a new channel just ahead of the supporting bars. The cutting machine whirls away in front of them, depositing the coal on the flexible conveyor.

As a new space is opened up, levers are adjusted to edge forward the entire conveyor and the roof supports. The shearer passes down the face again, churning away at the 'buttock' of coal, and pauses at the far end before it reverses and takes yet another *web* or slice of coal. As the conveyor moves forward to its new position, the unsupported roof behind it collapses into the *gob* or waste area behind.

At one time a face was on a twenty-four hour cycle: one shift cut the coal and fired explosives to break it up; the next shift (the *colliers*) loaded the coal on to the conveyor belts; the third shift (*packers*) packed up the roof behind, while *panturners* dismantled the conveyor belt and re-assembled it nearer to the face. Nowadays, it is all one operation. Cutting and loading go on at the same time and the roof is supported by hydraulic props.

It is possible for these various operations to take place in the one shift and each shift can, in theory, become a coal-getting shift. In practice, two coaling shifts are worked, followed by one for maintenance.

This ripping machine digs out the roadways leading to the face

Shotfiring

The powerful shearer loader has removed the need for shotfiring on the face, but 'shots' are still used where a completely fresh tunnel is being made through solid rock.

The deputy or shotfirer first tests for the presence of gas. When he is certain that the air is free from gas, he packs the explosive tightly into the hole that has been drilled for it. This hole must be free from cracks that might cause it to blow out dangerously. Plastic packs of water or gel (jelly-like substance) seal the shot in position.

Everyone retreats to a safe position at the end of a long cable at least 20 metres away, and preferably more. A lookout is posted to prevent anyone approaching from the other side. The shot is then fired and the water and gel mist which arise help to suppress the dust and fumes. Those fumes that remain are drawn up and out of the upcast shaft by the ventilation system (see chapter 3).

The size of the flame in the lamp shows how much gas is present

Packing explosives into the hole

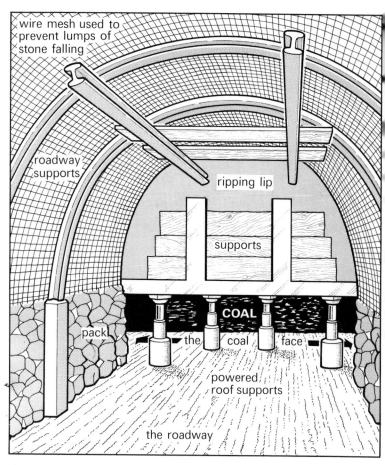

A diagram of the face lip, showing the packs.
Though the packs start off 1.5 metres high, and help to control the movement of the roof, they cannot for long carry the enormous weight of rock above them. Within a few weeks, the packs will be crushed down to half their original height

Supporting the roof and face

The props and bars for supporting the roof while the coal is being cut are now an integral part of the armoured conveyor. But further support is needed for the roof in areas where the coal has already been cut.

At the side of the roadway, packs have to be made which extend five metres into the gob on either side of the roadway. These packs are made of fallen stone and debris and look rather like a drystone wall. The space behind the wall is packed solidly to the roof with debris and dust, sometimes blown into place by a mechanical stower.

The packs have to be airtight to force the air along the face and down the *Main Gateway* (the main tunnel). Air taking a short cut across the gob, instead of going along the face, would cut off ventilation there, and probably cause a fire in the gob itself as air was drawn over the coal that had been left behind.

The old method of supporting the roof, with wooden props

The modern method of supporting the roof

Even the strongest steel girders cannot hold these tremendous forces. They can and do protect the area above men's heads, but as the weight increases they are pushed into the ground or the ground heaves up between them. This waste material has then to be dug out until the floor of the roadway is level. *Dinting* is the miner's word for this process.

Hydraulic props are also used. A hydraulic prop consists of two steel tubes, one inside the other. The larger one acts as the base of the prop. The upper tube contains a hydraulic fluid reservoir and a pump, operated by a lever, which forces fluid under the base of the upper cylinder. This pushes the upper cylinder against the roof. The lever is pumped several times more until there is a resistance of about five tons—the 'setting load'.

When the load reaches a pressure of 20–25 tons the liquid is allowed to flow back into the reservoir chamber and the prop lowers slightly. If the pressure falls again, the prop remains in its new, slightly lowered, position. This obviously makes it much more flexible than the old timber prop or the simple metal prop.

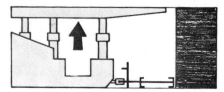

1. The powered roof support before the shearer takes a slice of coal

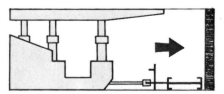

2. The shearer has passed. Now the hydraulic ram pushes the conveyor belt forward into the new space

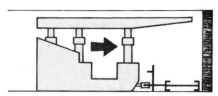

3. One roof support is lowered, while its neighbours support the roof

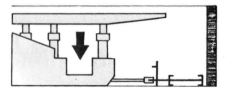

4. The roof support is moved forward and raised again

The control panel of a remotely operating longwall face (ROLF)

If a hydraulic prop needs to be moved, the miner can retreat to a safe position and by hauling on a chain he can make the prop telescope. It can then be pulled clear of the resulting fall of rock.

Fully mechanised coal faces advance so quickly that many men would be required to operate the hand-worked hydraulic props. So self-advancing supports have been devised which use the same method, but are worked by a pump which is situated on one of the road-ways leading off the face.

A hydraulic ram first of all pushes the armoured conveyor forward into its new position next to the face. The five or six hydraulic props each have a cantilever bar to support the roof. They are lowered and pulled forward into their new position. Then they are raised to touch the roof again. All this is done without great effort by a miner operating valves.

On a *remotely operating longwall face* (ROLF) the self-advancing supports can be operated by a miner who is not even on the coal face at all. He works in the roadway leading off the face, so no-one needs to be in the danger area on the coal face when props are being moved.

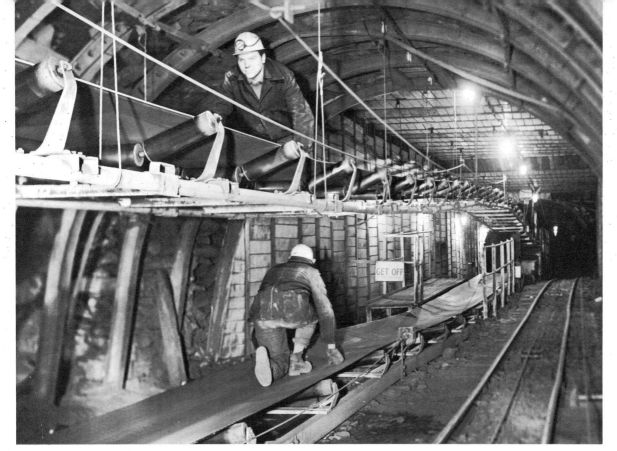

Some modern conveyor belts can now carry men

Haulage

Mines vary a lot, but they all need an efficient system of transporting the coal from the face to the pit head, and of transporting men to and from the face.

In some mines, coal comes straight from the face onto conveyor belts, which take it direct to the pit bottom. There it is poured into a measuring *hopper* and transferred to a *skip*, holding ten tons of coal. The skip is then wound to the pit top. There it is off-loaded on to another conveyor belt which carries it to the washeries and processing plants.

Men are not normally allowed to ride on coal-carrying conveyor belts because of the danger of accidents. In some pits, however, there are special man-riding conveyor belts. These are designed to take men to their work quickly. Speeds of up to 30 kilometres per hour (km/h) are reached instead of the more usual 8 km/h. Collieries like Lynemouth extend up to 8 kilometres under the sea and it is obviously important for men not to waste a large part of each shift in travelling to and from the coal face.

The main conveyor belt

A 100 hp diesel locomotive. Notice the wire mesh on the ceiling to prevent stone falling on to the roadway

Many collieries use powerful diesel engines to pull mine-cars. There are over 1000 diesel or electric locomotives in use underground, all specially maintained so that they do not give off too many dangerous fumes or sparks.

Diesel locomotives cannot normally go right up to the coal face. The seam may be at an angle, or up a slope, and diesel locomotives cannot cope with gradients steeper than 1 in 15. Or there may be 'green' ground, which means ground which is settling down into its new position after a layer of coal has been extracted. The area of green ground extends approximately 300 m back from the coal face, before it becomes reliable 'settled' ground. Rails cannot be laid on green ground.

Fast conveyor belts, wider and stronger than the face belts, receive the coal from a face belt at a transfer point. They deliver a river of coal into mine cars at a loading point and the cars are then taken away by diesel locomotives, or battery-powered tractors.

On any gradient steeper than 1 in 6, even a conveyor belt is useless because coal rolls back down it. Here the old system of rope haulage is still used.

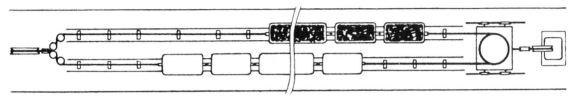

A *run* of tubs (a train) is usually attached to the rope by a special clip or, if it is really steep, by a chain. A runaway truck on these steep slopes is a frightening thing, but *manholes* (cavities cut into the side, out of harm's way) are provided at intervals along the roadway. A runaway truck gives some warning by the noise it makes and manholes have to be provided every 20 m on steep roads.

In a rope haulage system, trucks are pulled along by endless ropes wound on drums, with empties on one truck and full trucks on the other

Some roads in Lancashire have gradients of 1 in 2. It is a hard day's work just to walk them.

The engine room of a rope haulage system

The ventilation system of a mine. The arrows show the direction of the air flow

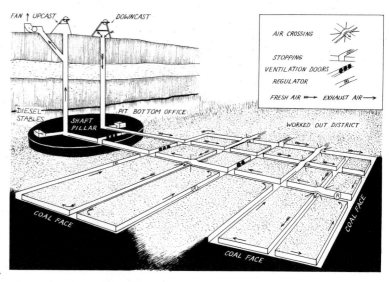

A ventilation duct, drawing air into a 'dead' tunnel where air will not naturally flow

3 Ventilation

Each mine must have two shafts in case an accident happens in one of them. These shafts carry telephone wires, pipes for compressed air, electricity cables, pipes up which dirty water from the workings is pumped and pipes which carry clean water for dust suppression, fire fighting and other purposes. All these pipes, wires and cables have to be led along roadways right up to the coal face.

These two shafts are also an important part of the ventilation system. Fresh air must reach all parts of the mine, or the men would suffocate. The draught of air goes down the *downcast* shaft, round all parts of the mine, and back up the *upcast* shaft.

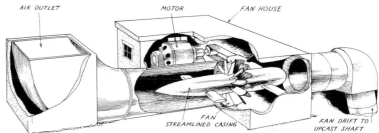

The upcast shaft has a huge fan at the head which sucks stale air out of the mine. A system of ventilation doors prevents air from rushing down the downcast shaft and straight up the upcast shaft. It is forced to take the long way round, so that all parts of the mine are ventilated.

Where a return airway or roadway crosses an intake airway, one roadway has to go over the other in a sort of flyover so that the two air-streams do not mix or short-circuit, and take the quickest way to the upcast shaft, leaving part of the mine without air.

If one road crosses above another it is called an *overcast*; if it crosses beneath it is called an *undercast*.

Some ventilation doors have regulators in them which allow the correct amount of air to pass through. The doors are arranged in threes so that there are always two doors shut tight. If someone coming the other way tries to open a door at the same moment that you have opened another door, the air pressure is so great that he will not be able to open it.

As you pass through the doors you often move from one 'climate' into another. The air on the downcast side is cool and fresh (in winter this fresh breeze can be very cold indeed) and on the upcast side the air is very warm and may contain traces of gas. Miners passing through the first set of ventilation doors often leave behind articles of clothing to be picked up on the way back.

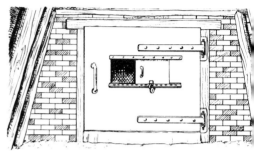

Ventilation door (top) and a regulator in a ventilation door

Measuring the air flow with an anemometer

How the air flows over the brattice cloth

Stoppings are built into disused roadways so that air cannot pass down them

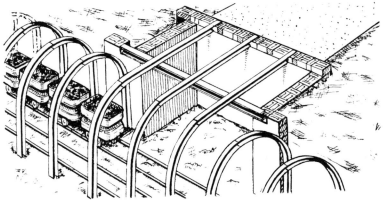

For each 40 m in depth the heat increases by 1°C. The average depth of British mines is approximately 450 m and the deepest mine is approximately 1050 m.

There are some *headings* (new tunnels through the solid rock) through which the air cannot be drawn, and it has to be forced to penetrate by means of a PVC *brattice cloth*. This catches the current of air and forces it into the 'dead' parts. A brattice cloth can also be used to direct the flow of air into the roof, to carry away pockets of gas which may have collected there.

Where a really strong flow of air is required down a lengthy heading, an auxiliary fan is used to boost the air flow. If the flow of air is speeded up, the amount of dust is diluted by the extra air. But if the flow of air becomes too fast, extra dust will be picked up. A balance has to be struck

As well as clearing away dust, the flow of air carries away diesel fumes, explosive fumes and the deadly gases such as methane or 'firedamp' which are produced in a mine. Heat and humidity are also reduced by this flow of air.

10 VENTILATION DEVICES

■ 1	MAIN FANS
■ 2	AIR CROSSINGS (EXPLOSION PROOF)
■ 3	AIR CROSSINGS
■ 4	STOPPINGS (EXPLOSION PROOF)
■ 5	STOPPINGS
■ 6	DOORS
■ 7	REGULATORS
■ 8	PACKS
■ 9	AUXILIARY FANS
■ 10	BRATTICES

4 Safety in mines

General precautions

In 1906, 1129 men lost their lives in pit accidents. This figure has been reduced nowadays to about 50 killed a year and nearly 400 seriously injured. Coal mining is therefore still a highly dangerous occupation, so the safety of the men is a vital consideration.

The Mine Manager himself is responsible for safety in his mine. Each colliery has its own Medical Centre with a qualified nurse to deal with minor injuries. In addition, there is usually a First Aid man who regularly checks all stretchers and first aid boxes kept underground.

Every colliery has a fully-equipped Rescue Room in case a full-scale attempt has to be launched. Working miners are trained in the use of special breathing apparatus, so that they can form rescue teams. The colliery's own rescue service is backed up by a Mines Rescue Centre which serves several collieries and has a permanent staff on call 24 hours a day.

Practising first-aid. Some of the tunnels below ground are quite as steep as this

This mask can be used to protect the miner from carbon monoxide gas.

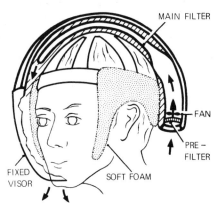

MAIN FILTER

FAN

PRE – FILTER

FIXED VISOR

SOFT FOAM

Face workers can wear this special dust helmet

Men called 'samplers' travel the roads, taking pinches of dust at different points. The samples are analysed in the colliery laboratories

The peril of dust

Modern machines create noise, dust and fumes at the coal face. Dust has always been a great problem, but modern research has shown us just how dangerous it is. The coal face, with the shearer loader working at full blast, is a very noisy and dusty place. The whirling picks of the shearer loader cut coal into small particles and some into fine dust.

At one time finely powdered coal was not required. Householders and coal-fired railway engines wanted large pieces for their fires, not 'slack'. At some collieries, coal dust and small pieces were left behind in the gob. Some colliery managers insisted that colliers (coal-getters at the coal face) used forks to load their coal so that they left the dust and small pieces behind. But now finely powdered coal *is* required. Power stations are among the largest users of coal, and they blow fine coal into their furnaces.

However, if a miner breathes too much of this finely powdered coal it can seriously harm his lungs. Every effort is made to prevent dust polluting the air he breathes. In the sweaty heat of most coal faces, masks are very uncomfortable to wear, but they are available for anyone who wants to wear one.

Water is the best controller of dust, so water jets play continuously over the point of the cutting picks, to damp dust down at its source. Curtains of fine spray are produced to clear the air. Clouds of dust are created wherever coal is transferred from one belt to another, or into mine cars for transport to the pit bottom. Water jets at all these points help to control dust.

The roof of the coal face, often consisting of coal, grinds on the metal canopies which protect the miner. This is another source of dust and nowadays every effort is made to prevent it from falling between the metal plates into the air which the miner breathes.

Not all dust is equally harmful. Larger particles of dust are stopped by the nose or throat and do little harm, but very fine particles pass into the lungs and make a small scar in the lung tissue. When too many of these scars are caused, the miner is said to be suffering from *pneumoconiosis*. In serious cases his breathing becomes difficult. He has to retire from heavy work and his life can be considerably shortened.

Not all miners suffer equally from the same amounts of dust, just as not all men who smoke cigarettes suffer from lung cancer. Research is going on to find out just who is especially at risk. Nowadays there are regular checks on the state of a miner's lungs so that action can be taken before it is too late. Mobile medical units throughout the country test miners' lungs by X-ray.

Air samplers called *allutriators* are hung in dusty places. These 'breathe' the air in much the same way as a man. Heavy particles which would not affect the miner are trapped at the first stage, corresponding to the nose and throat, and the fine, damaging particles of coal and rock dust come to rest on a special filter plate. At the end of a measured period of time the filter is taken to a laboratory and weighed. The increase in its weight is a measure of the amount of dust breathed in.

The National Coal Board (NCB) has established the Institute of Occupational Medicine at Edinburgh, where scientists research into the problem of pneumoconiosis and other throat and lung diseases of coalminers. Teams of investigators are permanently stationed in industrial centres, conducting surveys into the risks from dust and fumes.

A gravimetric sampler. A miner who works in especially dusty conditions may carry a smaller 'personal gravimetric sampler'. It is usually fixed to his cap lamp and keeps a close check on the amount of dust he is exposed to

Dust barriers above the main roadway conveyor

Explosions

There is yet another danger from coal dust—the danger of explosions. Finely powdered coal dust, when ignited, can cause fearful explosions, as bad as any caused by gas. Clouds of fine coal dust can explode if touched with a naked flame. A slight explosion of methane gas near the coal face could trigger off an explosion which could tear along the whole roadway, if precautions were not taken.

These explosions can be prevented if coal dust is mixed with stone dust. So bags of stone dust, looking rather like flour, are scattered along the roadways. Stone dust barriers are also erected. These are shelves loaded with stone dust stretching across the width of roads and resting lightly on brackets fastened at each side. If a methane explosion occurs, the shock wave knocks down the shelves. The clouds of stone dust then prevent the *gas explosion* from developing into the more severe *coal dust explosion.*

An experimental coal dust explosion at MRDE (see page 54)

Firedamp explosion in a Victorian mine

Sparks

Fires can be caused by sparks from the mechanical picks as they cut into stone, and electrical machinery sometimes sparks. The equipment is carefully checked to make sure that explosions cannot be caused this way. All equipment has to be tested by the Safety in Mines Research Establishment at Sheffield or Buxton. Because of careful testing, electricity is no longer a serious cause of explosions.

Gas

Coal seams produce several different types of dangerous gas, called *damp*. *Firedamp* or methane causes explosions. *Blackdamp* or *chokedamp*, a mixture of carbon dioxide and nitrogen, is a very heavy gas which can cause suffocation. *Afterdamp* also causes suffocation because it contains carbon monoxide and is particularly dangerous because you can neither smell it nor see it. *Stinkdamp* is the miners' name for hydrogen sulphide which smells like rotten eggs.

Some seams produce more gas than others and the deputy has to check for the presence of gas throughout his district, particularly at 'dead' points in the roof, or 'corners' where gas collects because the air does not circulate freely. Testing is always carried out before 'shots' are fired. It may be necessary to get rid of the gas by directing air into these collecting points by means of a hurdle of brattice cloth (see page 26).

When the concentration of methane gas (firedamp) is greater than $1\frac{1}{4}\%$, electrically driven machines must not be used. In gassy seams, such as the Barnsley seam in Yorkshire, compressed air may well be preferred.

A cage of canaries may be kept in the Rescue Room. If someone has to go on rescue work where there is a danger of poisonous gas, he takes with him a canary in a special cage. The canary, which has a faster rate of breathing than a man, soon becomes unconscious if there is any gas. The miner then knows that he must leave that area immediately. The canary is revived by oxygen supplied from a cylinder fitted to its cage.

Each colliery also has its own 'gas chamber' where men and officials carrying gas-detecting lamps can be trained in their use.

Testing for gas

Using a canary to test for gas

Communications

Mines need a good communications system. In one mining disaster an underground paddy train, operated by rope haulage, was pulled into the smoke of a fire near the coal face. The guard of the train had no way of telling the engine driver (who was more than a kilometre away) what was happening.

The train went on its way into the smoke, going too fast for the men to jump off. The engine driver at last saw smoke creeping into his engine room. Thinking fast, he hauled the train back out of the smoke. By this time, many of the miners were dead from suffocation. If the guard had been able to communicate by radio, this would never have happened.

Radio waves do not travel far underground, but a radio cable can be laid along the roadway. This 'leaky' cable can pick up a radio signal. The guard carries a mobile hand set and is in constant touch with the engine driver. This new device is in use at Cadley Hall colliery.

The cable strung along the roof is a 'leaky' radio cable

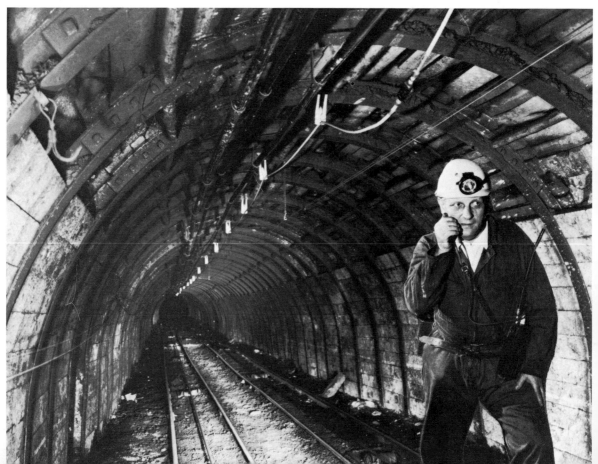

Lighting

Lighting, too, is becoming more efficient. In most pits the roadways are lit as far as halfway to the face. Some pits have lighting right up to the coal face, and there are even coal faces which are lit along their whole length. The lights are fixed on the advancing line of roof supports. On a face lit only by the cap lamps of one or two miners, it is all too easy to move the huge machines without knowing another miner is there, and the man may be crushed against a wall of coal.

Lighting has been introduced to a few coal faces which makes them safer as well as helping the men to cut more coal

Surveyors and engineers

Among the buildings on the surface is the Surveyors' Office. Plans of the underground workings are made here and must be brought up to date every three months. It is vital also to know the whereabouts of old workings, to prevent an inrush of foul air or water. The new workings must be kept to their own territory and not cut into another colliery's coal or, even worse, break into their tunnels, which would upset the ventilation of both pits.

Faults in the strata (where the coal seam has slipped out of place, owing to movements of the earth) are also indicated on the maps and the steepness of inclines through these faults is also shown. The surveyors' work has to be very accurate.

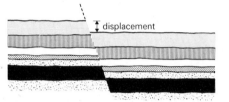

A fault

A laser unit, fastened in the roof of roadways, is one of the modern developments that has assisted the surveyors in their work. This unit sheds a continuous, accurate beam of light which acts as a guideline for keeping roadways straight and level.

The Colliery Engineers (both Mechanical and Electrical), have their offices at the pit head. They are responsible for machinery, including the very important cage, winding ropes and engines.

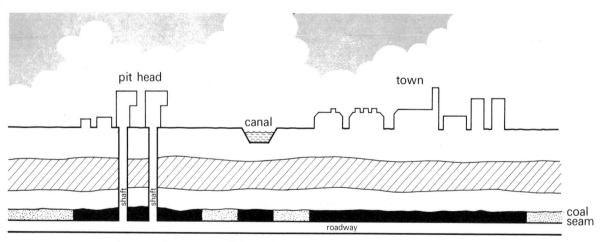

coal left for support

coal cut here

When the coal is extracted, the ground above sometimes sinks slightly. This is called subsidence. The surveyors leave pillars of coal under large buildings on the surface to prevent damage

A mining village of the 1920s

5   The mining village

In the past, miners were often cut off from the rest of the community. Mining villages, often the size of small towns, tended to be a long way from other villages and towns. A young boy almost always followed his father down the pit. Any other kind of work involved a journey to a distant town and travelling was costly.

Almost everyone earned his living from the pit—even the shopkeepers. When times were bad they were bad for everyone in the village. When they were good, everyone was better off. This bred a feeling of 'togetherness' which is still strong, even though the pattern of life has altered.

A modern mining village

The Miners' Welfare Club

The miner spent some of his evenings at the Miners' Welfare Club, where all the members were miners and the talk was often of mining matters, and then he went home to his colliery-owned house. His holidays he took with his fellow workers. When the pit shut down for the holiday many of them stayed at the same seaside resort.

Miners have always been keen on sport and many young miners have become successful professional footballers and cricketers. Dog racing, fishing, pigeon racing, brass bands, even leek-growing and choral singing have been very popular, in different parts of the country. They still flourish, but an even wider variety of interests has been added to the list.

Nowadays, modern transport has changed some of the feeling of isolation, but it is still true to say that there is a special feeling about a mining community. The rhythm of the pit, with its coming and going of men on three shifts a day, dominates the life of the village. In the old mining areas the pit head stocks still stand at the end of the street and great spoil heaps of earth, shale, rock and waste materials from the mine, dominate the skyline, while subsidence cracks houses and even, at times, wrecks the farmers' land.

However, the modern miner probably takes his wife shopping by car in the nearby town. He drives home instead of having to tramp on foot or ride his bicycle through all weathers in the middle of the night.

Miners and their children fifty years ago

Miners playing rugby

The Durham Miners' Gala. Each year all the miners in the area march through Durham carrying these magnificent banners

Some miners, of course, still follow the old pattern of life but their sons are much less likely to do so. They can travel quickly to nearby towns to a variety of jobs. They may go to college or university and leave the area. Sometimes they return to a job with the NCB as a qualified mining engineer or scientist.

Increasing numbers of miners live away from the colliery village and travel in daily to their work. As mining has become mechanised, fewer people are needed.

Although there are many influences which appear to be changing the life style of mining communities, there is little sign that the independent spirit of the miner is changing. Perhaps there is something special about the very act of going down a pit to earn a living that makes a man feel differently towards his job and feel specially close to other men who share his way of life.

6 How coal was made

Fossils

Fossils in coal are the remains of fresh water creatures which lived millions of years ago. Coal was formed about 250 million years ago in the Carboniferous Age, when hot swampy forests existed in a climate very different from today's. These forests consisted of great fern-like trees, which were inhabited by lizard-like creatures, insects and lower forms of life. Layer after layer of dead trees in a great spongy mass contained the remains of creatures which had lived and died there.

This spongy mass was gradually covered by sand and mud which hardened into rock. In time, the layer of vegetation was buried under millions of tons of rock. The great pressure of this rock compressed and condensed the vegetation and changed it into coal. This change was also helped by bacteria.

The coal seam may be buried a kilometre or more beneath the surface and the sea has possibly been over the same place several times, leaving its traces in the various layers of rock and sand covering the coal. While it was there, sand (brought down to the sea by rivers) was laid down layer upon layer and now exists as seams of sandstone many metres thick.

Dead plants and animals in the swampy forests were later affected by the pressure of the rock above them. Their skeletons changed into different substances, but many kept their shape unchanged and are found in coal as fossils

The swampy forest may have looked like this. Fossilised tree stumps are sometimes found under the coal seam

Shellfish fossils

Coal measures

The layers of sandstone, shale, clay and coal so formed are known as the Coal Measures; they are the upper part of a series of rocks called Carboniferous or coal-bearing rocks, which are thought to have taken about 75 million years to lay down.

The Coal Measures can be as far down as 3000 m in Great Britain, but 600–900 m is more common. The coal is usually found at the bottom or in the middle of the Coal Measures. There may be over a hundred seams of coal, but many of them are unworkable for all but special purposes as they are less than 60 cm thick. Some are only a few centimetres thick.

There are places in England (in Kent, in Durham and in Cumberland) where there is coal a long way out under the sea, and there are some very high mountains in the world, forced up by earth movements, which have coal seams high up in them. In Peru coal is found at 4500 m above sea level, which is the equivalent of half the height of Everest.

Mountains are perpetually being worn away by wind, rain and ice. As they are worn away, coal seams are exposed and it was in these surface seams, usually in hilly districts, that coal was first discovered. A seam of coal is often named after the place where it outcrops, or comes to the surface. For example, one seam is called the Barnsley seam because it is found near the surface at Barnsley in Yorkshire.

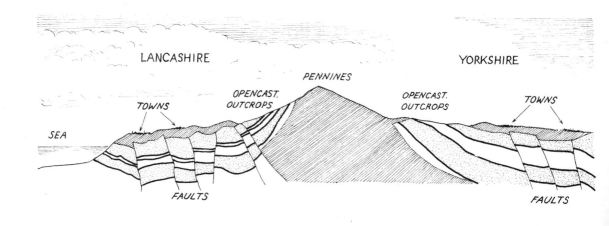

Peat

Peat used to be dug up by hand and used for fuel

Coal is not being formed at the present. At the mouths of great rivers in equatorial regions great masses of vegetation are being laid down, and this was the way the old seams were produced. But it is unlikely that all the conditions necessary for the creation of coal will ever again exist together at one time.

A substance rather like coal is formed in bogs and marshes. It is called *peat* and is formed from the mosses which grow and die in the bogs, gradually forming thick layers of brown spongy material which can be cut, stacked and dried, and used for fuel.

Peat is found in Scotland, in the Lake District and in many moorland and marshy areas. In Ireland, where there is little coal but much peat, there are five power stations which make electricity by burning peat. If peat is buried beneath a great deal of rock for millions of years, it turns into coal. Even then the coal seam would not be very thick, for the peat is pressed to about a tenth of its original thickness.

The South Staffordshire coal field has a seam 10 m thick, and in Australia there is a seam 250 m thick, so you can work out how much peat there must have been originally. Most seams being worked in Britain are 1.5 to 3 m thick.

Machines now cut peat for use in some power stations in Ireland

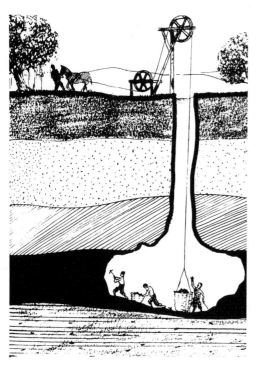

A bell pit

Loading coal into a barge 1796

7 The history of coal mining

Early coal mining

Coal was first used as a fuel by men who picked up lumps of coal from exposed seams (*outcrops*) at the sea edge or on hill sides. When these surface seams were exhausted, men constructed *bell pits*. These were primitive shafts in the ground which hollowed out into a bell shape at the bottom. When the pit became dangerous, because of the difficulty of supporting the roof, it was abandoned and another pit was dug nearby.

An improvement on this system came when the *room and pillar* method was adopted. Large blocks of coal were left so that the roof had support and 'rooms' or empty spaces were left between the blocks of coal.

As early as the fourteenth century, pits were dug with small shafts and tunnels as in a modern pit, though bell pits continued for a long time after this. Of course, there was no machinery and the coal had to be carried on people's backs or drawn on sledges to the bottom of the shaft. Then it was pulled up the shaft on ropes, or carried on the backs of miners, who climbed up a series of ladders.

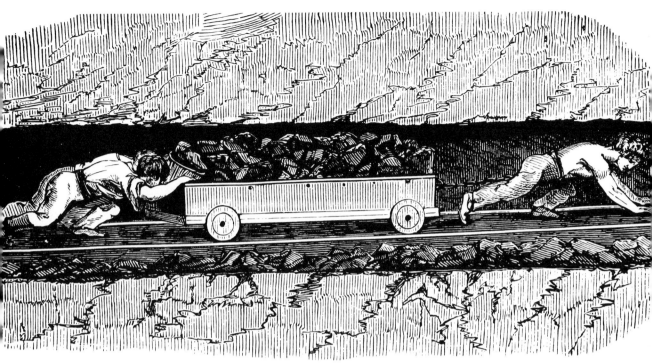

Children working in a mine in 1842

In some places, for example near Newcastle-upon-Tyne, coal used to be mined in *drift* mines. These are mines which go down to a comparatively shallow seam of coal, not by shaft but by a tunnel, which slopes down from the surface to a coal seam.

On the North-east coast of England, coal could even be picked up on the shore where the sea had washed it out of outcrops in the cliffs. As the mines were near the sea, the coal was sent in trucks down the rails to the waiting ships, called *colliers*. The miners did not need horses to haul the coal; it was downhill to the sea, and the heavy coal wagons going downhill were linked to a chain which pulled the empty wagons back up the hill. The ships took the coal to London and to other cities on rivers or near the sea.

Collecting coal on the sea-shore, probably after a storm had uncovered a coal seam beneath the sea

It was common for women and children to be employed below ground, carrying heavy baskets of coal and hauling tubs along rails, going on all fours like animals. An Act of 1843 put a stop to the employment of women and children *under ten* underground; in 1887, the Coal Mines Regulations Act said that boys could not work down the pit under 13, or at the surface under 12.

A pit pony. A few mines still used horses and ponies even in the early 1970s

Robert Stephenson's Rocket, one of the first really efficient steam locomotives

In the main roads of the pit, horses and ponies were used for many years to haul trains of tubs. As recently as 1955, over 10 000 ponies were at work in mines but these have all gone now.

Introduction of machinery

The first steam engines were invented and used by Thomas Newcomen in 1713. He used them to pump water out of pits, and so mines could be dug still deeper into the earth. James Watt is one of the greatest names in the history of mining machinery. In 1769, he patented the first steam engine which could drive a wheel. His steam engine was soon used instead of Newcomen's to pump water out of mines. In 1784, he invented a rotary engine which could wind coal out of quite deep pits.

The first man to make a steam engine which moved along iron rails was Trevithick, but one of the first really efficient ones was Stephenson's *Rocket*, which could go up to 35 miles an hour. This was a development of his first locomotive, built in 1814 to haul coal from Killingworth Colliery to the docks, 15 km away.

Mechanical haulage underground began late in the 19th century; engines driven by steam, compressed air or electric motors were used to supply power for rope haulage systems. This meant that the engine itself did not move but it supplied the power for pulling a rope to which tubs could be clipped.

The first successful mechanical coal-cutters were made by William Firth of Sheffield and used in mines from about 1850. They were powered by compressed air. By 1900, coal-cutters powered by electricity were in use. The miners, who were proud of their skill with pick and shovel, disliked and distrusted these new machines for many years; they feared, quite rightly, that machines would reduce the number of jobs for men.

Early coal-cutting machine

From 1914 to 1947, the coal industry was generally in a bad way. Many pits were small and inefficient. Output was much lower in 1947 than in 1913. Oil was becoming a more popular fuel and world trade was generally slack, so that exports of coal were almost nil and the number of miners had fallen drastically. Only a massive programme of mechanisation could save the industry. This, in fact, has been carried out with remarkable efficiency.

A colliery about 1920

Nationalisation

Demonstration by the NUM in London

Until 1947, coal mines in Britain were privately owned. This meant that there was little national supervision of working conditions and most miners felt that they were ill paid and badly treated by the owners.

Serious strikes had occurred in 1911, 1921 and 1926, while the 1930s had seen widespread unemployment and wage cuts in mining areas. Many people felt that the industry's problems could only be solved by nationalisation, that is, by the Government buying the mines from the private owners.

This was done in 1947 when the National Coal Board (NCB) was set up to take the old owners' place as employers, to control coal mining and to carry out a big programme of modernisation.

The National Union of Mineworkers (NUM) represents the miners themselves, and their leaders negotiate with the NCB for improved wages and conditions of work.

8 Uses of coal

Early uses

Men have known for centuries that coal can be burned to give heat. Bronze Age men in Wales used coal to cremate their dead; the Romans burned a certain amount of coal, but the Anglo-Saxons made little or no use of it.

By the Middle Ages, coal's usefulness began to be recognised. Monks are said to have collected it on sea-shores and dug it out of shallow pits for use in their forges.

But for a long time coal was regarded as inferior to wood and charcoal; it did not burn so well as logs on an open hearth nor produce as much heat as charcoal for smelting iron. By Tudor times, however, as wood became scarcer, more and more people took to burning coal in their homes. Bricks became cheaper when coal, instead of charcoal, was used to bake them and more bricks meant an increase in houses with fireplaces and chimneys.

Glass ceased to be a luxury after glass-makers used coal in their furnaces; meanwhile, brewers, dyers and soap-makers found coal to be a cheap and plentiful fuel for their businesses. It was the invention of the coal-fired blast furnace in 1735 that made it possible to produce iron cheaply and set Britain on the road to becoming an industrial power.

Glass-makers began to use coal in Tudor times

These pictures drawn in 1644 show the different fire grates used then for wood and for coal

An unusual use of coal, as a material for sculpture. A very hard coal is needed for this

The invention of Watt's steam engine and the ever-increasing use of steam power for railways, ships and machines of every kind called for vast amounts of coal and the sinking of new pits throughout the 19th century.

It was found at an early date that coal had other uses besides providing heat and power. In 1792, William Murdoch discovered that coal gas could be used to light houses and street lamps; coal tar was another early discovery and in 1856 a scientist named Perkin found how to make a mauve dye from coal tar. From these beginnings emerged the astonishing range of by-products which we obtain nowadays from coal.

A poster printed in Edinburgh in 1842, advertising cheap coal brought by the new railway

The old way of screening coal, picking out dirt and rock by hand

A modern coal washery

Modern uses

The coal which comes up from the coal face is 'impure'. This means that it is mixed with shale, dirt and even metal. Some of this impure coal goes directly to power stations which have boilers designed to cope with the dirt. But most of it is sorted into three sizes, washed (to separate coal from dirt) and then graded into the various sizes required for different uses.

Some of the coal is specially treated. A whole series of *smokeless* fuels has been developed; they are usually made of coal which has been crushed, dried, heated, and then squeezed into shape. Smokeless fuels are largely used for open fires, room heaters and boilers in towns and cities. Specially treated coal also provides the coke essential to the steel industry.

A fantasy view of coal washing in the Middle Ages

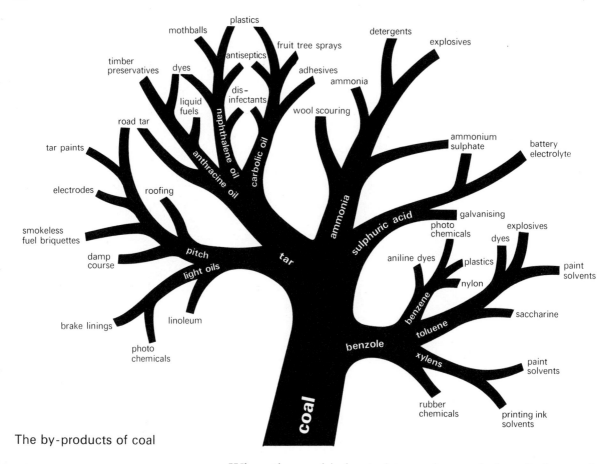

The by-products of coal

Making coke

When the coal is heated to make smokeless fuels, gas is given off. This gas is cooled and, in the process, tar is extracted, and so are ammonia and benzole. Surplus gas is sometimes supplied to the Gas Board. A whole series of different oils is produced from the distillation of the tar: light oil, carbolic oil, naphthalene oil, wash oil, anthracene oil, heavy anthracene oil and pitch. In turn they all produce different chemicals which are vital to modern industry in the production of:

fertilisers	dyes
antiseptics	wood preservatives
plastics	fuel
disinfectants	roadmaking tars
moth balls	paints
damp-proof roofing felt	

Ammonia is processed and used as fertiliser and in detergents and explosives. Benzole is used in making nylon, dyes, plastics, perfumes, photographic materials, saccharine, etc.

In some towns, district heating schemes enable coal to be used very economically. For example, Nottingham town centre is supplied with heating and hot water from one central coal-fired boiler house, linked with an incineration plant which burns the town's rubbish.

Coal can be supplied in big tankers and blown through a pipeline into the coal bunker. This is a clean operation, because the fuel is untouched by hand. But the most convenient way of transporting coal is to convert it into electrical power. This has been called 'coal by wire'. More than half of Britain's production of coal (73·5 million tons) goes to power stations and produces 65% of our electricity. The rest of our electricity comes from nuclear power and from oil.

Even colliery waste tips can be useful, ever since someone discovered that their black shale makes excellent base material for building motorways. At Pegwell Bay in Kent more than a quarter of a million tons of pit tip shale was used to reclaim land for an international hoverport.

Coal can be supplied by tanker and blown directly into a coal bunker

Lea Hall colliery, Staffordshire, is linked directly with a power station

9 Modern developments

Research

The Mining Research and Development Establishment of the NCB, at Stanhope Bretby near Burton upon Trent, employs about 800 people and carries out research into coal-mining problems. Nearby, at Swadlincote, it has a huge surface-testing site where prototypes (first examples) of new equipment are rigorously tested out.

The aims of this research establishment are to develop more efficient machinery and mining methods, so that production can be increased, and to improve the safety and working conditions of miners.

Testing new machinery

The central control room of a modern mine, with closed circuit television

A nucleonic arm at Cotgrave colliery

Machinery

The shearer loader with powered roof supports (see page 15) was a great advance, but the NCB is always seeking still better methods. A recent development is the *nucleonic arm*, which is an automatic steering system.

When a shearer is directed by hand the operator is likely, by mistake, to cut into the floor or into the roof. If this happens, the coal contains too much stone (as much as 20% of 'coal' coming out of the pit is stone which has to be removed at the pit top); the picks become blunted faster and blunt picks create much more dust than sharp ones (the dust from cut stone is even more harmful to the lungs than coal dust); picks make sparks when they strike stone and are the biggest cause of fires.

The nucleonic arm uses gamma rays to 'sense' the stone. Gamma rays pass through coal and stone at different rates; the machine measures these rates, works out where the stone begins and directs the shearer to avoid cutting into the stone.

Training for miners

One of the most important modern developments is the improvement of training facilities for miners. A young miner who enters the industry at the age of sixteen no longer simply goes straight down the pit to work with his father or an older man, picking up experience as he goes along.

A colliery training officer is responsible for all training arrangements at the colliery. After a general training programme, a newcomer is then placed under the guidance of another miner for 20 days of close personal supervision. However, the colliery training officer still visits him regularly at his place of work.

His first job is usually on haulage work, under the supervision of a haulage corporal who is in charge of transport. As he becomes more experienced, he moves to another job and eventually to the coal face.

Under a National Training Scheme, mining methods are taught at one of 45 centres. Apprentices learn electrical and mechanical engineering and this is followed up by practical experience at their own colliery.

Apprentices at Seaham mining training centre

Opencast mining in South Wales

Opencast mining

Although longwall mining is the most common mining method today, other methods are used when they are more suited to the geological conditions.

Coal can still be obtained from near the surface and modern developments have made it possible for opencast mining to be organised on a vast scale. First the top layer of soil, subsoil and rock is removed (to be replaced later so that the land can return to farming) and then huge draglines move vast amounts of coal away to waiting lorries.

'Big Geordie', which operates in the North-east, is the biggest walking dragline in Europe. The bucket of this machine can hold up to 50 cubic metres—as large as some single-decker buses. 'Big Geordie' is owned by a private company, not by the NCB, but the NCB has its own opencast workings, producing about ten million tons of coal each year.

The bucket of 'Big Geordie'

10 Modern coalfields

You can see from the accompanying map the extent of Britain's coalfields. Some areas which have produced large amounts of coal in the past have now become worked out. Today, two thirds of Britain's coal comes from the Midlands and the Yorkshire coalfields.

One of the most important seams is the Barnsley seam which outcrops near Barnsley in the west and slopes away to the east, getting deeper and deeper as it goes across Yorkshire and out towards Lincolnshire. This produces high quality coal and is between two and four metres thick. Much of the seam has been worked out, but a large area near Selby has yet to be worked. The Parkgate, Dunsil and High Hazel are other seams in this region.

In the Leicestershire coalfield, where good geological conditions make machine mining easy, output has exceeded $3\frac{1}{2}$ tons per man per shift. Many of the latest experiments have been carried out in this area because it is near MRDE at Bretby (see page 54).

Immingham terminal, where coal is loaded onto ships

A boring tower in the Firth of Forth. The tower is being used to search for undersea coal seams

The Northumberland and Durham coalfields have long been famous. The proverb about taking coals to Newcastle confirms this. Many of the old pits are now worked out. (These pits were named after the wives and daughters of miners and coal owners of the 19th century: Bessie and Mary, Lady Anne and Emma.) The miners now travel daily from their villages to great new pits on the coast where coal seams extend under the North Sea. There are at least 550 million tons of coal under the North Sea and already at Westoe the workings extend five kilometres under the sea bed.

Sea boring towers have been successful off the coast of Durham, but off Northumberland the sea is deeper, making drilling more difficult. Geologists think there are large reserves of coal there.

The search for more reserves of coal is continuing; the outstanding discovery so far has been the Selby coalfield.

This seismic survey team makes explosions which create shock waves. They can tell what kind of rocks lie beneath by the time the shock waves take to travel through the earth

Selby

Beneath the Plain of York, and probably stretching even up to York itself, is a whole new coalfield which is as large and as important as the oil discoveries so far made in the British sector of the North Sea.

To make the most of this new coalfield, the NCB will bring together all the latest engineering techniques that are at present scattered throughout the coalfields of Great Britain. At Selby they hope to avoid the problems of older coalfields, since every detail will be planned well in advance.

Automation, mini-computers, and a conveyor system with 30 kilometres of wire rope, will send an unending river of coal up the slope of the drift mine. Great new haulage engines will power the vast conveyor belts, delivering coal direct to waiting trains. At half-hourly intervals these trains will take 80% of the new-found wealth to three great power stations already existing at Ferrybridge, Drax and Eggborough, enough to supply one fifth of the electricity needed in Britain.

Examining the results of the seismic survey

This power station near Selby will use coal from the new coal field

The present plan is to produce five million tons of coal a year from this field. Eventually, ten million tons may be produced by only 3000 men. At the moment it takes 19 Yorkshire collieries to produce a similar amount of coal with 15 600 men.

The NCB has promised to take care not to spoil the countryside. Ventilation and service shafts, and the mine exit itself, will be camouflaged, for example among trees. No vast spoil heaps will be allowed to mar the landscape. Subsidence will be carefully controlled to avoid spoiling this low-lying countryside, a land of rivers, canals and drainage works, some originally made by Dutch engineers in the 17th century.

These two pictures, before and after, show how it is possible to reclaim land damaged by coal mining. The spoil heaps were removed and the land made fit for houses and for farming

Coming away from the pit head
after a shift

11 The future of coal

The plans for Selby make it clear that coal remains a
most vital raw material. Yet only a few years ago some
people were saying that coal mining was a dying
industry. Oil was cheap and plentiful; open fires were
going out of fashion; the diesel engine had replaced the
coal-burning locomotive and the steamship was obso-
lete; experts prophesied that atomic energy would soon
supply us with cheap electricity for homes and factories.

Since the early 1970s the position has changed dramati-
cally. Oil has suddenly become very expensive and,
although new oil-fields are being developed, it seems
clear that the world's total supply of oil will not last for
many years. Atomic power stations have so far proved
disappointing and coal remains the most important
source of supply for Britain's output of electricity.

Fortunately, Britain's coal reserves are thought to be
sufficient to last for more than a hundred years and
mechanisation of the coal industry has been so successful that coal can be mined quickly and efficiently. In
1947, it took 703 000 miners to produce 184 million
tons of coal—262 tons a man. In 1973, only 268 000
miners produced 130 million tons—473 tons a man.

Mechanisation has increased efficiency, but it is important to remember how much we owe and will continue to owe to the men behind this success story—the miners. Their work is safer and better paid than ever before, but mining remains a job that calls for skill, toughness and courage.

Booklist

Mines and Men, Tom Ellis, Educational Explorers, 1971
Power, R A S Hennessey, Batsford, 1972
Behind the Scenes in a Coal Mine, John Newell, Phoenix House, 1964
An Introduction to the Coal Mining Industry, C J White, Colin Venton, 1971
Mine Worker, S Cox, Kestrel, 1975

NCB publications—contact NCB Public Relations, Hobart House, Grosvenor Place, London, SW1X 7AE: they have a range of booklets, wall charts, etc.

The entrance to a drift mine at Barnsley. Notice the large ventilation fan top left, and the steep slope of the tunnel down to the seam

Index